In My Own Last Words

In My Own Last Words

**INSIGHTS SHARED
BY THE DYING**

Christiane zu Salm

PRECOCITY PRESS

Copyright © 2021 by Christiane zu Salm

All rights reserved. No part of this book may be used or reproduced in any manner without written permission from the author and publisher.

Editors: Deborah Steinberg and Julie Simpson
Translated from German by Elisabeth Lauffer and
Edna McCown
Creative Director: Susan Shankin
Cover Designer: Elizabeth Lenthall
Cover Image: Collage by Raphael Danke
Precocity Press, Los Angeles, CA

This book contains material protected under International and Federal Copyright Laws and Treaties. No part of this publication may be reproduced, distributed, or transmitted in any form or by any means, including photocopying, recording, or other electronic or mechanical methods, without the prior written permission of the author, except in the case of brief quotations embodied in critical reviews and certain other non-commercial uses permitted by copyright law. For permission requests, email the publisher at: susan@precocitypress.com

ISBN: 978-1-7377235-7-8
Library of Congress Control Number: 2021919946

First edition printed in the United States of America

CONTENTS

Author's Note	vii
Dying to Live	1
Insights Shared by the Dying	27
Exercise: Write Your Own Obituary	75
Example: The Author's Own Obituary	79
What the Dying Can Teach Us	85
Reviving the Lost Art of Grieving	95
Acknowledgments	103
Recommended Reading	105
About the Author	107

AUTHOR'S NOTE

THIS BOOK IS A collection of insights that people shared with me shortly before dying, as they looked back on their lives. Its first edition was published in German and Taiwanese in 2013 and spent six months on the best-seller list in Germany.

The creation of the English version with American-only insights was well underway when the global Covid-19 pandemic broke out. It felt vitally important to include reflections from people dying of the virus. Within my circle of friends, many had loved ones who were, sadly, gravely afflicted with the disease. My friends kindly arranged for me to speak with them, even if only very briefly, before their admission to the hospital. We used FaceTime and WhatsApp audio calling. Tears were shed, both theirs and mine, on every call.

During this pandemic period, upwards of four and a half million people worldwide have faced the reality that life can end in the blink of an eye. Most have been robbed of the opportunity to say their goodbyes and pass peacefully from this world. Their friends and family have been denied access to them, denied the ability to hold their hands, stroke their faces, or impart messages of forgiveness, gratitude, and love. This isolation has extended to those who have died of causes other than the virus, as health and safety precautions have prevented their loved ones from accompanying them in person in their final moments.

Although we all must learn to accept death, whenever it comes, rarely has dying been more inhumane than as the result of Covid-19.

This book is dedicated to each and every person who has lost a loved one to this horrible virus, and to all who were unable to say goodbye with dignity.

— Christiane zu Salm
October 2021

"When people think you're dying, they really, really listen to you, instead of just waiting for their turn to speak."

— CHUCK PALAHNIUK, *Fight Club*

DYING TO LIVE

THIS BOOK IS NOT about death, but about life; life as viewed by those in their final days, life as considered through the lens of dying.

As an end-of-life caregiver, I collect oral reflections from people nearing the end of their lives. "If you could write your own obituary," I ask them, "what would you say?" Initially, most people are reluctant to share, but once they let themselves speak freely, they speak with a degree of authenticity and truthfulness that is profound and moving, both for themselves and their loved ones—as well as for anyone who reads these insights.

Regardless of gender, race, or class, most members of Western societies do not enjoy discussing death. Humankind has not cracked the code for dealing with our fear of death, and death remains the most mysterious aspect of life. While none of us can live every day as if it were our last, especially not when we're young, in the rush of our daily lives and our planning for the future we can lose sight of — or never take the time to think about — what's truly important in life or what our existence means. Artists and philosophers tackle these topics, but most people prefer to avoid them.

I'm trying to get a better grasp on these questions while I still have the chance, and I think death — the end of life — is a useful tool for doing just that. I often picture death as a still, like those used to make liquor: Buckets of life experience are poured in at the top and work their way through the contraption. The distillate drips from the spigot at the bottom — the quintessence of an expired life.

A Change of Tune for the "Pop Princess"

When I first began doing end-of-life work, it was a total deviation from the path I had taken until then. For 20 years, I had worked in the glamorous world of international music and television management. I was the first woman in Germany ever to run a TV station, and I attracted attention for my combination of business and creative skills. Viacom then hired me to run MTV Central Europe, which I did for more than three years. After that, I worked for the international multi-billion-dollar media company IAC. The media called me the "pop princess," because in addition to my success in the media industry, I had also become a princess by marriage.

My work was all about life, youth, fresh content, and the future — always the future. I delighted in developing business models for the digital age. My guiding principle was to move forward, faster, further, with unbridled energy, passion, and the unwavering objective of double-digit growth. I was focused on yielding more and creating new content, never stagnating or stopping.

From the outside, my life was the picture of success. However, after becoming a mother to two girls, I started feeling stuck. I felt empty and burned out, and something inside of me — my innermost soul — was crying out for attention. I knew I needed to make a change.

The Avalanche

I'd been supporting social causes and volunteering for a long time, but that didn't mean becoming an end-of-life caregiver was the obvious next step. In a way, though, death and I were already on a first-name basis.

When I was six years old, my little brother died before my eyes in an accident. This tragic, traumatic experience was a defining moment in my life, a fact I didn't fully comprehend until much later, as an adult. Following my brother's death, my family lived life with a greater sense of intention and perspective. For instance, it wasn't a big deal if I got the occasional D in math, or if my best friend chose not to talk to me for a few days, because nothing would ever be as bad as the accidental death of a beloved child. And life does go on, somehow. All issues can be solved, somehow. Except the issue of death. It was a lesson my mother drilled into my head, and to this day, the shape my life has taken can be traced directly back to that pivotal experience. My ambitious career trajectory could even be viewed as a way of "seizing the day," making the most of my life on the terms society had taught me were important.

Many years later, death came knocking at my own door. While on a ski vacation, I was nearly killed in an avalanche that dragged me close to three hundred yards down the mountainside. I later learned that I was buried in a pile of snow more than ten feet high. It was a near-death experience. Hard to explain how it felt. I was like a white bath towel going through the spin cycle. Twice while I was under the snow, my inner voice called out to me, its tone neutral and measured: *You're going to die*. It was neither scary nor beautiful; it simply was. For a brief moment, I viewed the situation from a distance. Standing outside myself, I studied my body rolled up in this massive snowball. On an emotional level, meanwhile, I heard my little daughter crying, "Mommy! Mommy!" at every turn.

Then, 800 feet down the slope, the impossible occurred: the avalanche simply spat me out. I found myself sitting on a rocky ledge, skis gone, mittens gone, hat gone, snow pants torn. All death did was bruise my thighs.

That experience served as a reminder of how suddenly life can end. I have solemnly observed the anniversary of the avalanche ever since. I view it as a sort of second birthday—the day I was given the gift of life a second time.

Four years later, I realized I wanted to become an end-of-life caregiver. The realization simply came to me one day, fully formed. I felt the need to accompany dying people through the final stage of life. I was curious to learn more about life shortly before death. I wanted to tap into the dying process with all my senses, to see it, smell it, hear it, and touch it. I wanted to see if I could endure it. And I wanted to be there for those who would otherwise die alone.

Strolling Through Cemeteries

At first, the prospect of a complete career change was daunting. I couldn't shake the idea, though. It came and went, and I'll admit, I found it unsettling. Whenever there's something that's difficult to face, perhaps out of warranted fear or respect, I find a thousand other things that need doing first. I'll go so far as to tidy up my desk, file invoices, rearrange my bookshelves, or even defrost the freezer—which is really saying something.

One evening, though, I finally worked up the courage to type just two short words into Google: "Hospice Berlin." With a glass of wine beside me. Just to be safe. I had put this moment off for months. What was the worst that could happen?

Before I knew it, I was filling out an online application.

I heard back that I had qualified to be invited for a preliminary interview with two course instructors.

"So, why would you like to volunteer in hospice?" they asked me.

"I'm not entirely sure," I responded. "It's something I feel called to, perhaps because of the loss I suffered as a child when my little brother died."

I told them more about my encounters with death and the fact that I've always liked visiting cemeteries. Whenever I arrive in a new city, I visit one of its graveyards. I imagine the headstones talking to me. Who were the people whose memory is reduced to these meager details carved into their headstones? Did GRETCHEN GOLDSCHMIDT, 1904–1982, for instance, have a fulfilling life? What made her laugh? What made her happy? Did she experience failure? Did she have a good life?

What does it even mean to have a good life? It's a question I always come back to.

A WEEK LATER, I received an email from Lazarus Hospice in Berlin: I'd been accepted for a hospice volunteer training course.

That uneasy feeling returned. Wasn't the whole thing a bit creepy? Did I have it in me to see people to their deaths? Furthermore, the course was more than six months long and met on weekends and early evenings, times I reserved exclusively for my young children.

I can still back out, I thought. *I can say I changed my mind, that the schedule doesn't work for me, that I need to spend time with my family on weekends.* There was no lack of possible excuses.

After sleeping on it three nights in a row, though, my mind was made up: I would do it.

Cappuccino and Feelings

Would they have decent coffee for us, or only tea? I couldn't help but assume the other participants would fall into the "green tea drinker" category. I feel a pang of guilt whenever, cappuccino in hand, I encounter a green tea drinker. The fact that I prefer this delicious, albeit unhealthy, brew over a cleansing mug of hot tea always makes me feel self-indulgent.

To avoid this dynamic altogether, I drained my to-go cup outside the main entrance to Lazarus Hospice on Bernauer Strasse in former East Berlin—the exact spot where the Berlin Wall had stood. *Before the Wall fell, I bet people didn't spend their final moments thinking about it,* I ruminated, *and I'm sure those dying today feel indifferent to the fact that it's gone now. Oh, quit philosophizing,* I chided myself. I pitched the paper cup in the trash and, heart pounding, took the stairs to the designated room on the second floor.

I had to pass through the hospice on my way. There was a candle burning outside one of the doors. Someone had just died.

Silence.

What were the final words uttered in that room? Would I have the strength to stand by the dying until they drew their final breath? What would it be like to be in a room with someone who, just moments before, was saying something, asking something, requesting something? What would it be like to hold someone's hand knowing that, shortly thereafter, they would cease to exist? What could I possibly have to offer them?

These were the questions running through my head as I entered the classroom. A few other participants were already there; perhaps unsurprisingly, there were more women than men. We were a cohort of nine in total, along with two instructors. Lots of different faces and lots of different reasons for wanting to work in a hospice.

The course opened with a feelings circle. We passed around a rock, and each of us took a turn holding it and sharing how we felt. I'd never done anything like it before. I was coming from a world where feelings were negatively associated with sensitivity or weakness. The closest you might come to discussing your feelings was hearing someone tell you to "get your act together!"

I was also afraid of being recognized by someone in the group as the former "pop princess." Being emotionally vulnerable was not part of my image as someone who "had it all together" and appeared on red carpets smiling and radiating success. It is difficult to take a turn away from what society defines as "successful," especially when it entails sharing real emotions. Between my professional background and my upbringing in a family where expressing emotion could feel shameful, I wasn't sure how to approach the feelings circle. Like several others in our group, I was candid in my response: "This is uncharted territory for me. I'm excited to see what will happen in this course, but I have to admit, I'm a bit nervous, too."

That first day, I dismissed the feelings circle out of hand. Surely it was just some pop psychology drivel, right? However, I came to realize that sharing how we felt at the beginning and end of each training day wasn't a bad thing. In fact, it served to create an atmosphere of familiarity in the room, and any sense of uncertainty toward the other participants vanished. It's a lot easier to meet people on their level when you know what's going on inside them. To this day, I am still close with a couple of the people from my training cohort—even though it turned out that I was, indeed, the only coffee drinker in the bunch.

The Sacred Art of Listening

The most crucial aspect of our training was cultivating the capacity to truly listen to others, a skill that is central to doing end-of-life work. We spent an entire weekend practicing verbal and nonverbal communication. Have you ever sat with someone for fifteen minutes and listened with absolute attention and without responding in any way? That means no nodding, no signaling agreement or disagreement, no allowing your mind to wander, no chomping at the bit for your turn to talk.

This kind of listening, which demands laser focus on your conversation partner, is not as simple as it may sound. Our communications-centered, increasingly internet-focused culture encourages individuals to express ourselves constantly, and as anyone who uses social media can attest, it can feel like shouting into the void. When everyone talks constantly or feels the compulsion to respond immediately, we end up not actually hearing what anyone has to say.

When we make and hold space for another person to say anything—anything at all—knowing that they will be truly heard, we make it possible for them to simply be themselves with complete freedom, to resolve the aspects of their life that need resolution, and to make peace with themselves. To the dying, outside realities are no longer important. The only thing that matters is the dying person's inner path to release. That means that, as a caregiver, you neither offer solutions nor judge the feelings the person is expressing. All you do is open up a space for them.

To illustrate this point, one of the course instructors told us that a hospice resident once said to her, right before he died, "You know, you're the one person who didn't say, 'Don't be scared' when I said I was afraid of dying. That really helped. For once, I had the chance to talk about my fear. It was taken seriously."

Deeply listening is one of the greatest gifts we can offer a person at the end of their life. I'm not a perfect listener; I have to mindfully practice and cultivate these skills. Training in the sacred art of listening is an ongoing, lifelong process. However, it is a transformative practice that benefits not only those near death, but the listener and all the people in the listener's life as well. I have experienced the positive impact of cultivating the capacity for listening in my own life, and I believe it is a skill that has the power to change the world for the better.

A Hands-On Approach

It quickly became clear that our training wouldn't be very theoretical; the focus was much more hands-on. Through various exercises and role-playing scenarios, we gained an understanding of what the end of life feels like. As impossible as it initially seemed to me, I was repeatedly amazed at the degree to which this feeling could be simulated.

In one exercise, for example, we were asked to consider what was nearest and dearest to our hearts, then write it down on a paper necktie. After we hung the ties around our necks, the instructors moved around the circle with a pair of scissors and silently cut off each tie, word by word. My tie grew shorter, and by the time they reached the end of the phrase I'd written—"The love of my children"—and snipped it off, I felt I was being choked.

The exercise was called Letting Go. Is that something you can practice?

It turns out you can. Provided, of course, you're willing.

In another exercise, we took turns lying silently on the floor for half an hour to represent an individual in a vegetative state. Another participant would then touch that person. It was an intense experience. Lying there stock-still, you gain a deep understanding of how it feels to be at the mercy of another person. Try to imagine not being able to decide who gets to hold your hand, who gets to stroke what part of your body. The idea makes me extremely uncomfortable. All the more reason, then, to be extremely mindful when it comes to touching.

Another weekend was dedicated to forgiveness and reframing. One of the most important aspects of hospice work is helping the dying individual forgive themselves and others at the end of their life. This includes recognizing that even those parts of ourselves we consider "bad" have a good side, too. The caregiver's objective is to help the dying person see and accept this good side. This is how we create and hold space for a human being in their final days.

The more exercises we did, the more distraught I felt at the thought of facing dying people in real life. Would I know what to do—or not to do—at any given moment? What if I said or did something inappropriate? What if a situation pushed me to my limits and I started to sense, for instance, that I was letting sadness get the better of me? Beyond wondering how much I could endure, I questioned whether there was anything meaningful I could give these people.

There Is No Right or Wrong Way

I was able to let go of some of those fears after we worked with an exercise sheet that asked: *When do we say someone is dying? At what point does a person see themselves as dying? At what point do others see them that way? In a sense, we are all dying from the day we're born. That's the day our inexorable march toward death begins.*

In your own words, try to describe the point at which you would characterize a person as "dying."

I wrote: "Those individuals are recognized as dying whose bodies will soon cease to exist. Only then do outside observers recognize: Someone's dying."

As I wrote, I realized how long you could ponder this question and how many answers were possible. Don't we all start dying the day we are born?

As I suspected, everyone in our group wrote something different—and every response made sense. For the first time, I realized there was no such thing as an objective right or wrong way to providing hospice care. The best you can do is endeavor to approach dying individuals in a way that allows them the opportunity to reconnect with themselves.

Writing My Own Obituary

One day, the instructor introduced a new exercise: "I'd like you to imagine that you will die the day after tomorrow. Without question. Can't imagine it? Sure you can. You just have to want to. Grab a pen and paper and write your own obituary. You have fifteen minutes."

No way, I thought.

In the previous exercise, we'd been instructed to plan our own funeral, taking into consideration whether we wanted flowers on our grave, whether we wanted a grave at all, whether we preferred an urn or a casket, and whether we wanted a ceremony or not. If we wanted a ceremony, did we want it to be religious or secular, silent or with music, big or small? What memories or sentiments should be shared, and what would be better left unsaid?

I had no trouble at all with that assignment, because for one, church music is my thing—I love the sense of the infinite and the sublime it conveys, and I know every classical requiem by heart. And because I love cemeteries, I had no trouble envisioning a beautiful headstone or considering what trees and flowers I would like to surround me. I jotted down the specifications for my own funeral with the same breeziness I would jot down to-do lists or details for the handyman.

But how on Earth did they expect me to write my own obit?

I should note that, while American obituaries are often limited to a cursory rundown of an individual's vital statistics, in Europe they provide a more detailed narrative of the deceased person's character, life events, and personal philosophies. I needed hours, days—ideally weeks—to complete such a task—not to mention lots of quiet time alone to think things through.

Taking stock takes time, yet for this exercise I had just minutes to condense an ocean into a single drop of water. It was a tall order, one I balked at, until a voice inside me asked: *Hey, what's going on here? What are you, too full of yourself to do this? What do you care what people say at your grave? It's not like you'll be there to hear it.*

I realized, though, that I did care. In fact, it was the perfect opportunity to set the record straight on a few things without having to tolerate any contradictions or counterarguments. How convenient! The chance to let everyone know who the real me was. *How conceited is that?* was my next thought. *That's your ego talking. But why not? . . . Why should that matter?*

Cutting to the chase is always easier when you're running out of time. I decided against a résumé-style obit detailing my education, professional trajectory, friendships, relationships, children, hobbies, interests, and achievements. What should I do instead, though? List my top ten experiences? I'd spent long enough ruminating on my vanity (or lack thereof) regarding my death, and now another five minutes had slipped away. I couldn't waste any more time trying to remember everything I'd ever done, deliberating over which of the many chapters of my life to include, or weighing who or what was most important.

Beyond these swirling concerns, I still had to decide what I wanted to say to the loved ones I'd be leaving behind. I found myself coming up with lines like, "She would have loved to do more creative work, because she always suspected it was the best outlet for self-expression, and maybe she would have gotten around to it, too, if only she'd lived a little longer."

I felt a jolt of horror. What was I doing writing things like "would have loved" or "if only"? This was me I was talking about, the woman who embraced the Nike tagline "Just Do It" as a life philosophy.

And yet, what did I find myself doing now, in the middle of this exercise?

I had never realized how difficult it was to evaluate oneself. I had evaluated so many people at work, noting their strengths and weaknesses and compiling performance reviews for them—but when it came to myself, the task was far more difficult and unsettling.

After our time was up, each of us had to read our obituary to the group. For me, this was the most intense experience of the entire six-months-long course. It was extremely unpleasant, like a striptease of the soul—a narcissistic act of exhibitionism. It was embarrassing. *If only I could stuff the obit in my bag and tuck it away in a desk drawer,* I thought.

Hadn't I exaggerated just a little about all the great things I'd experienced and helped create? Was I truly as good a mother as I'd made myself out to be? On the other hand, weren't there spots where I'd downplayed my achievements? Where I'd given in to my tendency to sell myself short?

I would later learn that looking back at the end of life is not so much about judging as it is about accepting your life, without judgment. It's no easy task. Indeed, it is nearly impossible, because even saying that your life was "happy" or "tragic" is a judgment. Even so, it is important to look back at your life in a way that allows you to make peace with yourself and your choices.

As uncomfortable as the obituary exercise was, it packed a real punch. Never had I been confronted so directly and radically with the question of what mattered to me in life. I can't count the number of times I've thought back to that exercise, which provided the inspiration for this book.

Conversations With the Dying: "In Their Own Last Words"

I started toying around with an idea: What if people who knew they'd *actually* reached the end of their lives dictated their own obituaries to me, as we had been asked to do during our training? Would it help them to know an honest memory of them would be preserved? Would it allow them to decide how they wanted to be remembered and how they viewed their own lives in retrospect? Could it be a way to share things with their loved ones that they never could during life, whether out of shame, fear, or unrequited love? Why shouldn't people be given the chance to do their own thoughts justice before they died?

Standard obituaries printed in daily newspapers contain little meaningful information about the individual who died. The obit will include their birthdate and date of death, of course, along with a list of those family members they're survived by. Maybe there's an inspirational quote, a passage from the Bible, a line from their favorite song or poem, or even a few thoughts shared by the individual before they passed. Sometimes it's noted that their death was "sudden and unexpected," or that it occurred "after a long struggle" with cancer or another ailment. These details don't reveal anything about who the person was, though. The individual human life disappears between the Business and Arts & Leisure sections.

What kind of life was it, though? Was it successful? Was it happy or sad, or perhaps squandered? Did the person know how to lead a fulfilling life?

At best, we might learn this type of information about prominent public figures, whose deaths tend to receive greater coverage. We also know what the great philosophers, poets, and thinkers of the past thought; they often composed detailed accounts of what moved them in their final hours.

What about the cashier at the supermarket, though, or the municipal employee who lives next door? How do regular people view their lives as they approach death? Have they discovered the answers to life's big questions? Or are their insights more mundane? Who's to say what's mundane and what isn't, though? What proves important at the very end—the same things as always, or does something unexpected emerge? And what do people tend to remember as life draws to a close?

These questions were on my mind as I began to interview the dying, asking them who they'd really been in life. I spoke with nearly a hundred men and women, visiting them at home or in nursing facilities and hospices, listening to their reflections and transcribing the obituaries they shared. I conducted these interviews everywhere from major cities to the tiniest of rural villages, in both Germany and the United States.

My initial concern—that people would be reluctant to talk about themselves—proved unfounded, especially in the United States. Most of the patients I have visited as a hospice caregiver have been thrilled to meet someone interested in hearing their take on life. A handful preferred not to have their reflections written down, for fear of hurting loved ones by being too honest. Several were skeptical at first, then came around after hearing what others had shared.

EVERY INDIVIDUAL included in this book authorized the use of their text before publication. In some cases, I asked the person repeatedly if they wanted to edit their entry, lest it come across as too frank. Almost without exception, no one wanted a single word changed or sentiment softened. Therefore, with few exceptions, nothing has been doctored in these intimate reflections on life. Each obituary has its own language, its own dramatic composition, its own focal points.

For those who died of Covid-19, there unfortunately wasn't time for follow-up consultations. We were able to speak only briefly over FaceTime or WhatsApp. They all agreed immediately to my writing down and adding their obituaries to this book.

In some cases, names were changed at the request of the individual. Others did not want to include mention of their illness, in which case I have simply omitted this detail. Otherwise, no changes have been made.

INSIGHTS SHARED BY THE DYING

What Was the Truth I Was Ignoring?

HAD I ONLY been there for my mother when she got sick. But I would have had to give up my job, which would have been difficult for me financially. It would have meant looking into the abyss of uncertainty.

That's what I wish to leave behind: that I have regretted it for all these years. To this day I can't forgive myself that I didn't take care of her until the end. Why can't I make my peace with this? What was the truth I was ignoring? That I didn't love my mother unconditionally? Or perhaps that she didn't love me unconditionally and I had a "quid pro quo relationship" with her?

To be completely honest, I didn't really want to be there for my mother. When I was at university there was a situation in which I could have used her help and support. But she wasn't there for me. She didn't come. I was in college at Cal State in Sacramento, I was 21 and first I was sexually abused and then raped. Of course I didn't want to talk to just anyone about it, I was much too young and insecure. So I called my mother and told her, "You have to come. I can't do it alone." She told me on the phone that she was too busy with her work.

We never talked about this, but I damned her for it. Held it against her. And now I'm the guilty one. And so I would like to say: You have to make decisions in life that allow you to live with the consequences later. Since my mother died, I wake up almost every morning feeling guilty.

I took the coronavirus seriously from the beginning. From the beginning I wore a mask and practiced social distancing as well as I could. Disinfected every doorknob, every elevator button before I would touch them. African-American women, such as I am, are particularly at risk of contracting the virus. I lost my sense of taste a few weeks ago, then began coughing, then developed a fever. Which won't go away. I've cried a lot. Is my life really over? What if I end up in an intensive care unit and can't recover? What will happen to my family? I've never felt so helpless. The only thing that comforts me is the fact that I love my children and grandchildren without reservation and would go anywhere in the world for them if they needed me. And I know that they love me, too.

God, let me be well again.

— Olivia Williams, 75, Oakland
   Covid-19

After Rehab Came Covid

I got to know my husband in rehab. We both were drug addicts, since our schooldays. It's important in such a situation to have people around who understand you. And not only that, but people who have gone through the same thing as you. It creates an uncanny connection. For years I refused to go to rehab; I would start with it and then break it off. When I met Dave, suddenly everything changed. When he told his story to our group of nine, I started to cry. This damned struggle, the pressure from outside, the expectations of others to stop using and get back into life, and how it broke him. I stood up right away and put my arms around him. It was the most beautiful moment of my life. We fell in love and last year got married. We're proud of the fact that both of us have been clean for some time now.

My 25-year-old son Robert is a dancer, and we assume he's the one who transmitted the virus to me. Luckily, he exhibited only weak symptoms and only for a few days. We saw each other recently, on my birthday. We had a winter barbeque outside in the cold, so that we could protect each other. And now I'm deathly ill. At least that's how I feel. I'm extremely short of breath, and have a fever. When I tested positive for Covid I thought: *The party was a mistake.* But then I thought: *Maybe it wasn't Robert who infected me. Maybe it was at the supermarket or perhaps in the waiting room at the dentist's.* It's insane. Who would have thought that globalization would be firing back with a deadly virus? I just cannot imagine that after everything I've gone through, I'm going to die. Life is unfair. And yet I'm thankful. Yes, write that down. I'm thankful for the love that Dave gives me every day, and for my son's love. There's so much more to say, so much more to live, but I can't right now. Take care, you two. I love you both. Perhaps we'll see each other again. In case we don't, accept this as a memento. Oh, and something else: Dave, in the drawer in the bedroom you'll find letters, jewelry, and photos. Just in case.

—RICHARD GARCIA, 54, Miami
Covid-19

From One Day to the Next, It Can All Be Over

I feel extremely bitter, not about my life, but about dying young. Just last summer, we went on our annual family vacation, sailing in Greece. Everything was normal. Everything was fine, or as fine as any life can be. As always, I had my boss's ego to deal with at work, and was relieved to be away. As always, my wife Amanda would throw an occasional fit about who knows what, while Logan and Jason, our teenage boys, would argue over the sort of things you look back on as an adult and laugh about. Last summer, the issue was who got to be bowman; in other words, who got to be up front.

We looked through photo albums at Christmas and toasted each other, as always. *When it comes down to it,* we said, *we really do have a wonderful life. We can afford to go sailing in Europe every year. We're all healthy. Merry Christmas and Happy New Year!* The kind of things you always say.

From one day to the next, though, it can all be over. It's the kind of thing you don't fully understand till it happens to you. Although I can't say I fully understand it yet, either. I just brood about it constantly. Out of nowhere, I started getting bad headaches, worse than any I'd ever experienced, so I went to the doctor, who diagnosed me with an aggressive brain tumor. At age 49. You always hear these terrible stories about other people, but I never imagined it could happen to me.

And now I'm supposed to talk about how I view my life in hindsight, to leave something behind for friends and family. Looking back is hard, because it forces me to accept that I must let go of those things I'm looking back on. I'm not even sure I can reach that point before I die. But I want to try. For the sake of my wife and kids.

You all know I'm obsessed with fairness. I've been that way ever since I was a kid. Whenever I heard someone was being treated unfairly, I'd get involved. It often got me in trouble. I think that's why working for my boss has been such a struggle. He's desperate for praise and routinely sells the accomplishments and ideas of his subordinates—myself included—as his own. And he's selling these things up, as in, to his boss and the outside world. That isn't fair. I'm a computer scientist and have been working at a software company in Silicon Valley for twelve years. Two years ago, I developed a new marketing tool for a piece of company software, presented it to the group, and who do you think got employee of the month for it? My boss. I read the announcement in the elevator, where they always post who got employee of the month, and why. I was absolutely furious.

Unfortunately, I never dared to tell him how unacceptable I thought it was, because I was afraid of losing my job. I know it's cowardly, but who knows how soon I'd find a new one? Or if I could still afford the summer trips to Europe? My coworkers and I receive handsome commissions at that place. I've thought a lot about leaving the company ever since it happened, of course, but I've been torn between enduring injustice while providing my family with a comfortable life, and fighting for fairness at the risk of endangering my position. In any case, my work is very important to me.

I do, by the way, believe in life after death. I'm a devout Catholic—it's in the family. My grandparents went to church every Sunday. I love the ceremony, the grandiosity. Amanda and I went to Rome once and attended the Papal Audience. Besides my wedding, that was the most wonderful moment of my life. I felt Heaven was protecting me. Protecting me from all the adversity that can befall one.

I hope I can reactivate that feeling in time. I could really use it right about now. To just close my eyes and entrust myself to Heaven. One day, we'll all be there together again; that I know for sure.

—Trevor M. Smith, 49
 Brain tumor

Who Knows, Maybe I'll Be Reincarnated as a Whale. That Would Make Sense

Watching and learning—that's what I love in life. For instance, I love watching kids and their parents on the playground. The mothers' and fathers' behavior is often more interesting than the kids'. You can immediately see what's done out of love, or a heightened sense of care, or sometimes real fear. It's so difficult to strike the right balance in letting your kids go and allowing them to experience life with all its adversity and danger, but all its beauty too. Different things are dangerous to different people, just like beautiful things. More importantly, different things are *right* for different people.

I was diagnosed with ADHD as a little kid. For the first few years, my family didn't really know how to manage it. I was prescribed pills, but that didn't feel right. It took my parents a long time to understand what was right for me and what I needed. They weren't in agreement, either. They eventually sent me away from home, finally leaving me to my own devices. It was the only way.

I was sent to a fish farm on the Pacific. From one day to the next, I went from being a nobody just bumming around to being somebody who was needed. Being needed, yeah—that's important. Being part of something. I had to make sure the tanks were clean, salinity levels were correct, and the water was free from bacteria. We raised sea bream. When wholesalers came, I pulled the fish from the tanks and loaded them in crates onto trucks.

I actually wish I'd been born a fish. In the water you're free and light. There are no limits. You can just swim from ocean to ocean. There's no one looking to quiet you. Endless movement. That's my dream.

Why are people supposed to be quiet all the time? If they were, nothing would ever move. Sure, they say strength lies in calmness. There's much more strength in movement, though. And when there's something I'm passionate about, I *can* concentrate on it. How else do you think I could have worked at the farm for over ten years, fishing sea bream from those tanks whenever buyers came? So, it *is* possible. You just have to find what's right for you, though that's easier said than done. I feel lucky my parents figured it out for me pretty early on. Otherwise, considering my life is going to be over soon, I never would have known happiness.

I never wanted to have kids. I was afraid of the responsibility. Afraid I wouldn't make the right decisions for them. And afraid of sending them on a path that wasn't right. I know it's cowardly, but it is what it is. That's why I prefer watching kids and their parents on the playground and realizing that although it was the right choice for them, it wasn't for me.

Who knows, maybe I'll be reincarnated as a whale. That would make sense. My parents are Buddhists, and I ascribe to the same philosophies, so I believe in reincarnation. I sense that I came to this earth with good karma. I've stored up a lot of goodness and purged a lot of pain from my life. I'm not troubled by the approach of death. If anything, I'm going to close my eyes and call out to the ocean: *Come and get me. I belong to you.*

—MICHAEL STEINFELD, 49, Los Angeles

INSIGHTS SHARED BY THE DYING

Was That My Life?

My life has always been about adjusting. Simply adjusting to whatever happens. Like we do with the weather. When it's cold outside, we put a warm jacket on. If it rains, we open an umbrella. And that's how it is with life. When I was 16 years old my parents died in a car accident and suddenly I had to take charge of our ranch in Virginia. When all I wanted to do at the time was graduate from high school and go to college. I so wanted to be an aerospace engineer. But I had to adjust. There was no other choice. Then as a rancher I married and wanted children. But it turned out that my wife, Dorothy, couldn't have children. So I adjusted to that and now have no children. Real adjustment happens deep down inside. The acceptance of what is. But is acceptance the same as adjustment? Is it possible that I was just too reluctant to carry out my own plans? I could have sold the ranch, studied engineering at a later point, could have adopted children with Dorothy, and if she didn't want to, divorce her and create a family with another woman.

I think about these questions, lying here at home with Covid and increasingly exhausted. I have this shitty cough. Can you even understand me? My body hurts, my limbs hurt. My throat hurts and all the lozenges that Dorothy gives me don't help at all. But the key question is: Would the grass have been greener on the other side? Why am I only thinking of that now?

—Wayne J. Fancher, 66, Texas
   Covid-19

INSIGHTS SHARED BY THE DYING

*All I Want for Us to Do Is
Reminisce About Our Past*

Why can't married couples live apart when they get old? Jonathan and I have been married 54 years and raised three children, by which I mean to say, I raised them and Jonathan provided for us. We've been through thick and thin together. We traveled a lot, saw some of the world, and made friends along the way. We both enjoyed fulfilling careers as teachers. There was always enough money. We had a good life, and I really don't mean to complain.

The reason I *am* complaining, though, is that the good life we had is at risk of being destroyed. We may have sworn to grow old together, but the reality of that promise has proven very unpleasant. It almost feels like the period we're in now is rolling up all the good years of marriage we had and extinguishing them.

All I do now is take care of my husband. He's very sick. I can't even list all the things he has. What he fails to realize, though, is that I'm just as sick. All that matters is that he's being taken care of. *Jennifer,*

I'm thirsty. Jennifer, where's the TV remote? Jennifer, I need to use the bathroom. Then I cook something and he says he doesn't like it. So I throw it away, then he calls out: *Jennifer, is there anything to eat? I'm hungry.* All day he carries on like this, and at night too, when he can't sleep.

Where, amid all that, are you supposed to find the space to enjoy growing old together? It's hard to admit, but true: If one of us had died suddenly, the memories would have been better for the other. More pure. Untouched by the terrible burden of elder care that ruins everything. You become estranged. I always said that to Jonathan, too: *Let's protect our love and arrange for home health care. We'll meet up twice a day for coffee and cake and remember the wonderful times we had. Like the first time we went to Spain, when we got hopelessly lost in Seville, looking for the cathedral. If we hadn't lost our way, we wouldn't have met Juan, who later became the godfather of our children.*

Yes, that's how I picture a dignified end to a marriage. But you don't want that. You don't want strangers in the house. You want me to take care of you till death do us part. And for whatever reason, I can't defy you. Well, it looks as if I may die before you do. Considering what the doctors tell me, it seems pretty likely. Pretty soon I'll lose the ability to walk, and then I'll be the one requiring care until she dies. But don't worry, I don't want you to be the one providing it. All I want for us to do, my dear Jonathan, is reminisce about our past. At least one memory per day. It's the loveliest thing you can do at the end. It's the only thing.

—JENNIFER ANGERFIELD, 74, New York
Heart disease

IN MY OWN LAST WORDS

Better to Regret Something than to Be Sorry for What You Failed to Do

All of life transpires around interpersonal relationships. Above all, familial. For me, it's always a question of speed and direction. Just like in traffic. The earlier one marries, the more improbable it is that both partners will develop over the course of their lives at the same tempo and in the same direction. Even if you're traveling in the same car. In the beginning, when out of pure love you promise to stay together for the rest of your life, perhaps you talk about what things will look like in later years. I can hear myself saying: Oh, by the time we get that far, something will occur to us.

Unfortunately, after 22 years, nothing occurred to Jess and me. We married when she was 21 and I was 23. With all the dreams that one has of life then. And then we had four children, and everything was wonderful. Jess completed her training as a cosmetician, but never worked of her own free will, because she wanted to be there for the children. I was a truck driver. With enormous loads to haul. I earned well working night shifts. Our annual highlight was summer vacation, which we spent camping out in the same place every year. All four of our children can build a tent. I taught them that early on.

At any rate, the children no longer live at home, and so Jess has lost her life's work. Just at the moment when Bill, our youngest, moved to Ohio in order to train as a craftsman, I got an offer to work for Sterling in sales and marketing. Sterling previously belonged to Ford, and I was to work on marketing the F-650 Ford truck. A great opportunity for me. A particular challenge that really gave me a kick. From truck driver to marketing staff—not many achieve that. And the fact that this could happen in mid-life is something that never occurred to me.

But that's not the way Jess saw it. She asked me: "And what am I supposed to do all day?" For as a truck driver I worked shifts, and not regularly, so I was home a great deal.

I always told her that she should look for a new interest, it didn't matter what, even if it were raising cacti. Or knitting egg cozies. It didn't matter, the important thing was to find something fulfilling. She didn't want to pick up her cosmetic work. She didn't want to do anything except prevent me from taking up a challenge. "Why did I marry if now that the children have left home you no longer have time for *us*?" It was the greatest conflict of my life. I had to choose between my wife and my work. It was not an easy decision and Jess didn't make it any easier. From her viewpoint I was thinking only of myself, and from my viewpoint she was only thinking of herself. It was a mess. In the end I went with the opportunity offered me. And Jess accepted it. She still hasn't found a new pastime, it's true, but she didn't divorce me. We created so much together—to throw it all away just because one is suddenly thrown back on oneself would have been ungrateful. I said that to her over and over. Am I ever glad that Jess turned the corner! She goes to a fitness studio regularly, to a nail salon, gets together with her friends. And every Saturday night I take her to an Italian restaurant. That's our new ritual.

But I've been in hospice here in California for a few weeks now. And soon it will all be over with my life. I'm very realistic about it. When I got the diagnosis of an incurable disease, I at first was intensely afraid. I had anticipated almost everything, but not that. I cried, despaired. Jess was wonderful, held me in her arms for hours with infinitely great tenderness. At some point I accepted the fact that I would die. How lucky that Jess was and is with me, my whole life long. Yes, it's my greatest good fortune that she didn't leave me back then. And our children are taking great care of me. If I have to die before my time, then it's a comfort that I'm not alone. I take my leave of you with my deepest heartfelt gratitude. Don't grieve too much for me, I seized my opportunity. One day you'll have the same chance, and please seize it. So that at the end of your lives you won't have to say: If only....

Better to regret something than to be sorry for what you failed to do.

—Dan Milton, 58
   Lung cancer

All the Pain We Inflicted on Each Other

I've been coughing constantly for five days straight. It's a strong and painful dry cough; I constantly feel the need to drink gallons of water. I've had a fever that has gotten worse for three days now. And I can hardly breathe, and talking to you is difficult. I feel weak. We'll have to take it slow, okay? When Stacy and Elizabeth, my two wonderful daughters, heard that I had a bad case of it, they came immediately. But they were careful to wear masks and stay at a distance. We didn't hug each other. But just the fact that they arrived right away and were with me for a few hours was a great help to me. I haven't seen them since, it would be too dangerous.

I coach a girls' soccer team in Florida; I retired ten years ago. Since then my marriage hasn't gone well, it slowly went downhill; actually I didn't notice it at all. Perhaps it was because I was at home too much, despite the volunteer work I do in the community, where I inspire girls and young women to succeed in their sports career. Now that I think about it, things weren't going so well even before

I retired. You get into your everyday routine and don't notice things if you're not looking closely enough. Our marriage apparently only functioned when both of us were out of the house a lot.

Particularly since we became empty nesters. Ted works at Walmart in logistics, and has much more to do now, with the pandemic.

A few years ago he told me he'd had a brief affair with a co-worker, which hurt me deeply. And that was it for me. I wanted to divorce him right away. I never thought he would cheat on me. And my parents were furious as well. Why did you even tell me, Ted? You could have spared me so much pain. And surely I you as well, for with our divorce everything was over. Somehow I regret that now. I miss you. Our closeness, our evenings snuggled up together on the couch, our parties in the kitchen pantry, which was so small we thought the walls would crack open. I could have forgiven you this sidestep. Should I die of Covid, send this to Ted please. And you have my permission to publish it. He should know that I still love him. I should have conquered my pride. I can only say it to you in this way: I ask for your forgiveness, Ted. I'm sorry for all the pain we inflicted on each other. If I survive this, we'll try again, okay? I'll cook you that ginger ground beef casserole again that you said no one could make as well as I do.

—Debra Smith, 58, Orlando,
  Covid-19

INSIGHTS SHARED BY THE DYING

*How I Wish I Had More Time
Now to Really Get to Know You*

Why does everything get so much more complicated and serious as one grows older? Does it have to be that way? Where along the way does one lose one's lightness, one's mischievousness, one's ability to live in the here and now? Children have that down, just aren't aware of it.

Until I arrived here at the hospital I was a bank clerk at JP Morgan Chase in California, responsible for more than 20 private banking staff members. A lot has changed in the last 10 years, today nobody needs talk to someone on the other side of the counter window. And yet I truly enjoyed my profession; it was always posing new challenges. As none of my constantly changing bosses gave me the boot, I take it that I've done a good job.

That wasn't the case at home, where I didn't do such a good job. My wife saw it coming. We married young, and from the beginning it was clear that we would have children, and that she would take care of them. She never had a problem with her role as a mother and housewife. This subordinate role never made her feel inferior.

God granted us three sons. The first, Adam, died when he was five years old—of a rare heart disease. I believe that our marriage is one of the few that survived something like this. We immediately went into therapy, which helped. Each of us had a couple of minor affairs during these difficult years. And it helped because it was always clear to both of us that we wanted to stay together. But to occasionally sleep with someone else in such a situation was a kind of relief.

And then Steven and Tom were born and everything was good, on the surface. Until Tom began suffering from depression at the age of 21. One morning he saw no reason to get up. He was at an elite university at the time, and we had every reason to be proud of him. He had to be admitted to a clinic, it was that bad. And then what was wrong with him emerged. He was suffering from the fact that I had always favored his brother Steven. And you know, it was true. I just never noticed it. Susan was always telling me this, so I should have recognized it. But I didn't want to. She always said: "Don't you see that you go to Steven's baseball games, but never to Tom's? That you teach Steven about sports and games with patience and purpose—but not Tom? That you visit Steven three times a year at college, but Tom maybe once, if at all?"

To be honest, the reason for this was that I saw Steven as the substitute son for Adam. He was very similar to Adam in personality. Extroverted, adventurous, smart. I went so far as to imagine that Adam continued living through Steven. So I could never let go of my dead son. Even though my therapist always told me how important that was. Not only for my peace of mind, but also for Steven's. I had inflicted a great burden on him. And never could see Tom for the wonderful young man he had become. I don't really know who he is, what he thinks and feels.

To Tom: How I wish I had more time now to really get to know you. But now that I'm deathly ill, it's too late. Despite that, I'm very happy that I at least have come to an understanding of all of this before I die. And that you know that I know what a huge mistake I have made. Please believe me: I didn't do it on purpose. I love you exactly as much as I love Steven. If you have children one day, you'll understand: Anything can happen, anything can get out of hand. From one day to the next, without your noticing. Or rather, wanting to notice. In my next life I'll do better.

   —Richard Dennett, 58
      Pancreatic cancer

INSIGHTS SHARED BY THE DYING

How I Longed for My Father's Approval

When I could still move, I visited my father's grave every Friday morning. Friday morning is a good time to visit a cemetery, because practically no one else is there. Everyone's probably preparing for the weekend, going to the hair salon and then to the market. You only see pensioners at the cemetery; in all my years I've never seen a child there. In any case, I stood at the grave of my father for 11 years, and each week I asked him why he never once told me when he was alive that he was proud of me. This question troubles me to the extent that I asked it aloud at his graveside. Three times in a row, which had a therapeutic effect. And that's why it was important to me to be alone and surrounded by several rows of gravestones. I felt better afterward. Even if he no longer could answer, it did me good to address his grave.

I knew that he was proud of me, only because my mother told me so. But she told me only after he had died. I was a senior teacher of math and physics at a college preparatory high school. My father taught math at a grammar school. So I clearly inherited my professional inclination from him. But I got further than he did. And I assume that he couldn't tolerate the fact that his son had attained a higher position in the same profession. Maybe he was even a little jealous of me. He apparently told my mother many times that he was proud of me, but I don't really believe it. Because he always acted exactly the opposite. In my head I go through all the times that we saw each other over the years. And now that I myself am dying, I have even more time for this. And I see how much time I still spend thinking about it.

He didn't congratulate me on passing my teaching exams, never attended a school celebration, even when it was just the summer festival. He never said anything appreciative, nor anything that was critical; he didn't say anything at all. Nothing about my choice of wife, nothing about teaching methods or mathematical formulas or school policy, nothing about salary possibilities in the public sector. It often made me crazy. How can someone go through life without taking any position at all? Maybe he did have an opinion and just never expressed it to me.

I even asked a number of his friends, and they all said to me: *Come on, Michael, we don't know what he thinks either. He just does his thing.*

How I longed for my father's approval. In retrospect it's clear to me that this unfulfilled wish was the most important thing to me. Nor could anyone else help me with it, that's clear to me now. There's no substitute for a father's pride in you. It's true, I think, that my students liked me. And I've almost always felt loved by my wife. But I never knew where I stood with my father. And now I regret that I never had the self-confidence to ask him. I could have asked, "Papa, do you find it good that I became a teacher too?" Or more directly: "Are you proud of your son?" But I never had the courage to, for fear of never getting an answer to this question that was so very important to me. As I never did to all the other questions I had. That's why it was so good for me to make up for it by asking him at the cemetery. A gravestone can't answer; but then, I'll never have to fear a hurtful reply.

And then there were the years when I decided that my father's respect and pride in me weren't important. In truth, however, it was important. At least I've made that clear before I die. We don't have any children to whom I could say: "I'm proud of you." But if we had had any, I would have said it to them regularly. Every Friday morning.

— MICHAEL MARINGA, 62, Minneapolis
　Leukemia

INSIGHTS SHARED BY THE DYING

You Must Opt for Life

I love my walker; I can use it for so many things. It's a shopping cart, stroller, chair, umbrella stand, and rolling suitcase all in one. Much better than a car. I go walking on the beach with it every day, here on the west coast of America. I'm here because I followed my ex-husband here; he lives around the corner now and has remarried. But that doesn't bother me, everything's fine. Before this we lived in Hawaii for 11 years. It was wonderful! We planted marijuana in the garden. I love the stuff, it makes you feel so good. It's also the best pain medication in the world. I always gave it to my daughters for their cramps, and it's wonderful in terms of my cancer. On top of which, it helps to dry my tears when something upsets me.

When you plant marijuana you have to be careful that it doesn't grow too tall. It's better to keep it low and far apart. The police can smell it. They have planes that can detect it. Once they showed up at our house, ripped up our plants and took them with them. But nothing came of it. I'm sure they took it home and rolled nice fat joints with it. Not a problem. We just planted more.

The first boyfriend my daughter wanted to marry tragically died. He installed lights and was working on an extremely high pole when he fell. He died instantly. Sometimes we're totally unaware of how dangerous life can be. I'm sure it wouldn't have been of any help if his parents or even my daughter had said to him: "Change your job, it's too dangerous, it could be the end of you." He wouldn't have listened to them.

Our children have to make their own experiences. We really can't protect them from anything. They might understand what we tell them, all of our advice that is equally frightening and loving, like "Be careful here" or "Don't do that, because then this will happen." But the truth is, they have to learn it for themselves. Basically, we can't teach our children anything about life nor protect them from pain.

Recently, my other daughter had a facelift. She's in her early forties. I asked her: "Why in heaven's name do you want to do that? Look at me, with all my wrinkles. What's wrong with them?" The fact that women today want to look ageless will cause them a lot of problems down the road. Because external and internal age diverge more and more as time goes on. But hey, why should I worry about other people. They'll discover it for themselves.

Following my second marriage, I was involved with Matthew. He was a great companion. We took fantastic bike trips together, down the entire coast, then we had a car and after that a van. We had a super time together, until he died, also of cancer. We came back from a trip and he felt pain in his spine, it turned out to be a lethal tumor. But Matthew wanted to go, he was ready. The single painful memory I have connected to his dying is that I should have given him more to drink. He didn't want to eat anymore, but he wanted to drink. I should have given him more water.

In terms of life's pivotal events, you only know much later what they are good for. That everything, no matter what it is, at some point and for whatever reason, proves itself to have been right—of that I'm sure. But I've often asked myself why we recognize this only in hindsight. Why not earlier, why not at the moment it happens? Well, life is like that. You must opt for life. Then everything will be okay, no matter what happens to you.

Please write down the following: After my body ceases to be, I don't want to be put in either an urn or a coffin. I'm against being put into a container. Cremate me and spread my ashes in the Pacific Ocean. Yes, that would be the right thing for me.

—Linda Goldberg, 75, Santa Monica
  Stomach cancer

INSIGHTS SHARED BY THE DYING

I Think Today is Thursday

When I was a baby I was taken from Romania to Detroit. My parents did this. We were being persecuted as Jews. I don't speak a word of Romanian, which is too bad. And so I have no connection to my homeland, I have no roots there and have never been there. My parents had no intention of teaching me the language, they were too busy worrying about our survival. I speak only English.

Despite this I have made the most of my life. I even think that this is easier for people like me than for most others. If you've ever been pushed to the edge, experienced, that is, what it's like to have to depend fully and solely on yourself alone to confront a perilous situation—it changes the way you look at life. You take it in hand, with no ifs, ands, or buts. Because there's no other choice you don't mull it over, you don't hem and haw about it.

After high school I joined two other girls from Romanian emigrant families and we opened a nail salon in Los Angeles. Nothing else occurred to us and we didn't know how to do anything. It brought in good money right away, and continues to do so today. That's what I love about America. No one judges you for what you make of yourself. I'm very satisfied with my life. Over the years we could rent a larger space, and we even had Hollywood stars as clients. I can't name any names for reasons of discretion, I promised them that and besides, it would be bad for our business. Most clients want their nails filed in the French fashion, filed straight across and not rounded. That looks better on film, they say. Otherwise we don't talk a lot, they're usually on their phones.

I wouldn't want the life of a star. They all live in a golden cage, whether they want to or not. Many of them aren't even aware what this has done to their freedom. If you asked them, they would all say, without a doubt, that they are extremely free. But freedom isn't only measured in money. I know what I'm talking about.

I have had cancer for a year now. And that gets you thinking differently about life, of course. Because suddenly nothing is a given. From one day to the next it's clear that your life will soon be over. I don't have a great fear of dying, to be honest. That might have to do with the fact that I simply can't imagine it. Look, I'm sitting here talking with you on this bench on the beach. To our left above us the sky is gray and cloudy, and right above, it's a brilliant blue. And you see the birds on the roof of that building? That's a flock of dark sparrows. And in the midst of them a big white seagull. What's it doing there?

A short while ago a person walking by asked which day of the week it was. I didn't answer her, because it doesn't matter to me. I think today is Thursday. What difference does it make anyway? In a week it will be Thursday again. But then there probably won't be a gull among the sparrows on the roof. And whether I'll be here or not, well, I don't know that either.

—Irina Sukovic, 70, Los Angeles
    Breast cancer

Nothing Unresolved

I can still breathe, still speak, though only in between coughing fits. Tomorrow they'll come and take me to the hospital, where I'll have a ventilator. They will definitely have one available soon, because so many are dying at the moment. I'm afraid that I'll also die of the coronavirus. But perhaps I'll make it. Plenty of people have recovered. But at the moment I'm coughing a lot. I'll try to tell you what my life was like, so that my family and friends know something about me. In case that I die. Even though I can't imagine that or want to. Who can imagine his own death?

You ask if there is anything in my life that is unresolved. Well. I've actually never thought about that. Not really. It was always important to me to provide for my family. It was something Elaine, my wife, always expected of me, and I believe that I always met her expectations. Our children went to a private school. Johnny Jr. is a successful baseball player. Nancy, my daughter, is a lawyer. But those are just the facts, which I don't have to leave behind.

Anyone who knows me knows these things. It's very hard for me to talk about my feelings. About what I feel deep down. But you know why I think there's nothing in my life that's truly unresolved? Because I think I can say that I always very carefully considered whether the choices and decisions I have taken so far derived from self-confidence and were not fear-driven. Yes, that's the secret. For example, when I left a very well paid job as a tax consultant in order to build my own business, it scared my wife. *What happens if you don't succeed and we don't have enough money to send our children to a good college?* I always took such risks and it always worked. I'm absolutely convinced that if you're self-confident rather than afraid you can accomplish anything in life. And that's why I'm at peace with myself.

I haven't made a will yet. Perhaps I should now. You never know. I'm someone who never imagined he would die. Since I became infected, that has changed. We're all so much more vulnerable than we think, and than we want to admit. Me, too.

—JEFFREY A. LEELAND, 49, New York
Covid-19

The Acceptance of What Is, That's the Secret

My salvation is that I became a Buddhist early in my life, I was only 22. I came to Buddhism through a friend. He took me with him once to his teacher. Everything that he said, and all of the books on Buddhism that I have read since, persuaded me immediately. For example, that Buddhism, in contrast to Christianity, never blames you if you do something wrong. Nor does sin exist as such. Instead, Buddha wanted us, as human beings here on earth, to continue to develop ourselves, not to have to pay taxes to the Church in the hope of some vague sort of redemption. That we wouldn't be around to take note of.

I work as a dental technician. Even as a little boy I enjoyed fooling around with small pliers and wires. So in that sense I'm in the right profession. You can't make a major career of it, it doesn't pay much, and there aren't many possibilities for advancement. But I never really considered that, because the price one has to pay for professional advancement can turn out to be very high. I'd rather advance within, if you know what I mean. And for that, meditation is great, and generally everything that Buddhist teachings have to offer. And then one doesn't need anything more, externally—not a bigger front yard, not a bigger house or a bigger car. My family has always understood this, because they also are Buddhists. I met Elaine, my wife, at a silent monastery. For an entire week we looked at each other before exchanging a word. And that week formed the basis for our entire life together: We understand each other without a word and blindly.

Whoever engages with Buddhist teachings learns one thing above all: to accept the river of life for what it is. That sounds easy, of course, though it is anything but. But in my opinion, it's the most important thing one can strive for in life: the acceptance of what is. Then life becomes easier. It helped me to better accept the fact that life is unjust. Yes, damned unjust. My older brother, for example, always got more attention than I. At school I was never picked for the better baseball team, the other team always won. My colleague at the dental clinic does the same work for better pay. I could list even more examples of unfairness. My point is that it doesn't affect me. I can accept it. I look at the good that has happened to me, and this list is much longer.

And so, despite my psychic pain, I can more easily depart this world. I'm absolutely convinced that I'll be reborn in human form. I've followed Buddhist beliefs long enough for that. And my family has promised to let me depart well. They won't call after me: *We miss you so much, Dad.* For that would be burdensome to me. For my wife Elaine I feel nothing but love and gratitude. Despite everything that was difficult in our marriage, we always focused on our love.

And I'm proud of the fact that our daughter Hanna grew up from the very beginning with these same values. She never complains about the fact that we couldn't afford to send her to an elite university. Nor that basically we never were able to make great financial advances. Spiritual advances, yes. And you, Elaine and Hanna, will come through life well with them. You don't need anything more to be a happy person. The acceptance of what is, that's the secret.

— DANIEL ARCHELUTA, 54, Colorado Springs
   Kidney cancer

INSIGHTS SHARED BY THE DYING

*I Don't Want to Leave Anything Behind,
Neither Money Nor a Message.
Except for This One:
Make Your Final Days Good Ones!*

I enjoy being here in the nursing home. I've wanted to come here ever since it became clear that I'm nearing my end. It's something I always said to my children, and even put it in writing. And now I'm here. Here I'm not a burden to my family and am myself unburdened. I don't have to take care of anything. No more linens to change, no more clothes to wash, no shopping to do, or cooking, no light bulbs to replace. Wonderful. Actually, it's like being in a hotel. I think that's the least one can treat oneself to before one dies. And I'm happy to spend my savings on it, instead of leaving it to my children. Money well invested.

On top of which, I have fun with the others here. We visit each other in our rooms all the time. None of us can move around so well anymore, so we use our walkers or wheelchairs to roll around in. There's even a clique that has formed here on the third floor, just like we did in the schoolyard. A gang. Vivian and Milli, Zack and Tyler and me. Everyone has a different bell on his or her walker so that we already know who's rolling down the hall. Vivian's bell is particularly clear, like a snowdrop in spring. You should know that Vivian and I are in love. It was love at first sight, and when considering that our end is near one could say: at the eleventh hour. It's just great.

You know, you have to approach your end with a certain lightness. That's what I'd like to say to anyone reading this after I'm gone. For everyone at some point will experience it. Of course, it's not great that one is old and sick. That you can't move around so easily anymore. That it takes forever to get out of bed. That you have to depend on the staff, not to mention being taken to the bathroom and given a shower. But you don't want to make the situation worse by constantly complaining. No, a little gallows humor is called for, and a concentration on what you enjoy: love, good food, good wine, and entertainment.

Yesterday, for example, there was a bowling tournament in wheelchairs and Vivian and I came in second. It was great fun. What should I tell you about my past life—how I earned a living, created a family, solved problems, overcame disappointment and managed conflicts?

Looking back is not for me. What for? I don't want to leave anything behind, neither money nor a message. Except for this one: Make your final days good ones! Load up on pain pills so that you feel nothing, and then have fun. Every single day, until your last.

— Frank Mason, 76, Santa Monica
   Bone cancer

EXERCISE: WRITE YOUR OWN OBITUARY

YOU DON'T NEED to wait until you're dying to write your own obituary. In fact, I highly recommend doing it now. Yes, right now. You will likely learn something new about yourself, and you may just decide that it's time to take a closer look at how you're living.

Set a timer for fifteen minutes and write—or record a voice memo—whatever feels most vital, most essential, to say about your life. Often, the greatest truths come from our innermost souls when our brains don't have too much time to second-guess what we're saying. What have you learned? What do you regret? What have you loved? What is still unresolved or painful? What would you want your loved ones to know that you haven't already told them? What has life been all about for you?

This doesn't have to be the definitive version of your obituary. You can update it and rewrite it as your life goes on. I have written several versions of my own obituary since I first drafted it during my training, as time has passed and I've grown and changed as a person. The version I've included here is the most current version, the one I would want to leave if I died tomorrow.

Write your own obituary as if you were going to die tomorrow.

After you've drafted your obituary, read what you've written. Resist the urge to edit out the parts that feel shameful, embarrassing, or too raw — these are the places where truth resides, and they are often calling out to be healed. What could you do to feel better about these painful things without denying them or hiding them?

Now ask yourself: What would happen if you shared your obituary with the people closest to you, not after you die, but, say, tomorrow? What might be healed, repaired, or strengthened in your relationships with them? What might they get to know and appreciate about you while you're still here?

What if you asked your loved ones to do this exercise as well, and then share their obituaries with you?

EXERCISE: WRITE YOUR OWN OBITUARY

Uncomfortable truths, old resentments, and unhealed wounds might be revealed. But that means there is an opportunity for healing while you are still here on Earth, a gift we can easily lose sight of in the rush of our busy, everyday lives. Those approaching death don't usually have the time to do the things they wished they'd done, to right their wrongs, or to heal the broken places in themselves or in their relationships with other people.

But you likely do have time.

WHAT IF THE RESULT of sharing these profoundly personal statements is that you and those you love are able to live fuller, more truthful lives and love each other more unconditionally?

Isn't it worth taking the risk to find out?

EXAMPLE: THE AUTHOR'S OWN OBITUARY

I Love You, Whomever You Choose to Be

After all I've been through, I am truly and deeply grateful. Most of all, I'm grateful that I've made it this far on my transformational journey. I've gone from merely surviving to not quite yet thriving, but to accepting. Isn't that a big deal? Coming from where I've been, it really is. I used to feel like I was running the race of life with an invisible handicap, while everyone around me was super fit.

Now, I'm ok. I'm at peace with who I am and with my wild journey.

I've never really shared with my beloved daughters what it took for me to be their mother. To show up every morning as strong and as positive as I possibly could, while most of the time I was falling apart inside. Please forgive me for my shortcomings. You must know I've spent my energy as consciously as I could on letting you be who you are and providing safety for you. To be there for your family while dealing with constant inner turmoil is almost impossible. It was only after I burned out and fell into a depression that I understood my responsibility to go and dig deep into myself. To find out how I'd gotten there—from having this outstanding career as a media executive to breaking down and feeling unfulfilled, unhappy, unaligned.

I am grateful that I became aware of what my task was on this Earth before it was too late, that I have been able to step out of self-victimization and take on the challenge of growing and creating meaning. The hardest part of my journey was finding the courage to show my scars, to show up as who I am: raw, vulnerable, wounded. It took me more than a decade! It wasn't just that I felt ashamed of being perceived as a has-been TV pop princess who used to be a successful over-achiever and now had lost my mojo. On a deeper level,

EXAMPLE: THE AUTHOR'S OWN OBITUARY

I was afraid because taking off my mask was lethal in my childhood. Showing how I felt—sad, angry, and fearful—meant the withdrawal of love and safety. It meant rejection and abandonment.

I consider the unconditional love I've given my daughters the single greatest achievement of my life. I love you two, whomever you choose to be. Even if I've erred on the side of unconditionality by setting too few boundaries, I am indescribably glad that I managed to break my own family pattern of narcissistic psycho-emotional abuse and conditionality.

I have faced my trauma and grieved the losses, lies, and lack of love I experienced throughout my childhood and adolescence. And I must say that I am proud of myself for all these inner achievements, for my ever-growing self-awareness, for going from craving love and belonging at the price of self-erasure to leaning into the void, for moving out of the fear of rejection and abandonment and into a place of fearlessness. For leaning into the not knowing, just surrendering and believing. That's how I feel right now, and it's a good feeling. I even don't fear my end.

I feel I have built up my capacity to live fully, which is the same as living fearlessly. I have found my inner stability and no longer seek acknowledgment or salvation on the outside. How liberating! And, I have helped many others grieve their losses and create meaningful lives in which they can be true to themselves.

Now, on my deathbed, I can say I have no major regrets. Of course, there are still a few, as there are in everyone's life. After I've understood so much about letting go, I would have loved to experience a relationship based on true love. Not the classic modern relationship, in which sooner or later, all the irrelevant bullshit around expectations, duties, roles, and daily conversations about who will take out the trash inevitably gets in the way. No, after my transformation, I set the intention to meet someone with whom I could enjoy a deep spiritual connection based on trust, compassion, and honesty. We would become co-architects of our common universe, help heal each other's wounds, love each other's scars, and fuel each other's inner growth. And we would co-create art! We would create a healing house with Zen gardens, a healing library, an art studio, a healing kitchen. We would have a family and community table and invite all those who wanted to heal

EXAMPLE: THE AUTHOR'S OWN OBITUARY

and become whole. We would put each other first and love each other at our worst.

I have tears slipping down my cheeks as I write this. But these are tears of deep gratitude, not sadness. I am certain the universe has not forgotten about me. It would be easy to think, "Why don't I get more time?" However, I believe in the Zen wisdom that there is no such thing as timing. There is only consciousness.

To my daughters: Do it better than I did. Choose your partners carefully. May you never need to chase love but always be given it unconditionally. You deserve no less. Thank you for being my daughters and for giving me the gift of always being honest about who you really are. Thank you for showing up raw. This is the only way to become whole. Don't change anything about yourselves, and everything will come to you with grace and ease. Go thrive with joy, and remember: No need to fear anything. You got this.

P.S. But never drink bad coffee.

—Christiane zu Salm, 55

WHAT THE DYING CAN TEACH US

ON A PERSON'S deathbed, their whole life becomes clearer than ever before. Everything they have suppressed, everything unresolved in their lives, comes to the surface. Especially the quality of their lifelong relationships: who is and who isn't showing up at their deathbed says it all. After listening to the stories of the dying for over ten years, I have distilled some lessons that the dying can teach us about life.

Carpe Diem: Start Living Life from the End

This is the single most important message I derive from my work with the dying. Every sentence I hear from them serves as an alarm clock: *Hey, wake up! Don't assume you're going to live forever!* The dying teach us to live in the present moment by making us aware that our lives are finite. They can be the best possible teachers in consciousness.

I envision my life from the end moving backwards, like Benjamin Button, the fictional character created by F. Scott Fitzgerald and brought to life in film by actor Brad Pitt. Born as an old man, Benjamin Button ages backwards, growing younger and younger, until he dies as an infant. Metaphorically, the story invites us to look at everything from the perspective of the end of life and let it inspire us to live more fully in the present.

It becomes easier to settle disputes, to reach out to others, to forgive, and to repair our relationships when we imagine what it would feel like if the people we are not at peace with were run over by a bus tomorrow, or died of Covid-19. What do we want to say to someone but have not dared to, out of shame or fear? Which honest conversations with those we are close to have we put off because they make us uncomfortable? Envisioning our lives from the end allows us to diminish our regrets, to grow and to be truthful, before it is too late.

We must live life NOW, while we still can.

The Gift of Perspective

Every minute I spend with a dying human being, even on the phone, gives me the gift of perspective. After I return to my life and my everyday duties, nothing really matters anymore — the deal that fell through, the repair person who never showed up, the employee I was annoyed with for delivering something late, the shoes that were sold out in my size, my daughter taking out her bad temper on me, the printer breaking (again!).... The philosopher Alain de Botton draws a connection between the high levels of anxiety experienced by many people today and a loss of perspective. We often don't know how to place a disturbing event — a missed phone call, a friend's betrayal — within a context that is suitably large enough to see it in perspective. So, turning your eye to the end of life definitely provides such a sizeable context. As long as someone close is still alive, we can still make peace with whatever happened between us. We can still communicate. All sorts of annoyances shrink to their proper size, and I can keep them in their place instead of letting them overwhelm me. This allows me to focus on the parts of my life that are truly important to me.

An expanded perspective also leads to greater resilience. It is easier to bounce back from failures and disappointments when we can see them in their proper context; they lessen and even vanish when they're part of the bigger picture.

This gift of perspective is why I think everyone would benefit from doing hospice work for at least a couple of weeks at some point, and listen with their full attention to what the dying have to say.

Wiser Decision-Making

Beyond expanding my perspective, listening to people facing mortality has made me rethink the lens through which I approach my own life. Automatically, every person's reflection makes me ask myself: *Have I become as aware as I possibly can up until today? Have I been a good partner and mother like this person has? Have I put my energy into the right things? Have I chosen the right people to let into my life? Am I comfortable with who I am right now? What regrets do I have? Have I been successful in my career at the cost of those around me? Have*

I been focusing enough on what's important? Each time I reflect on these questions is an opportunity to check in with myself about whether I'm in sync with the decisions I'm making in my life.

The idea of "rethinking" or "reevaluating" our lives can feel abstract or disconnected from our practical, day-to-day routines. However, our everyday experiences are a direct result of the decisions we make. When we truly think about the impact of our decisions, we can make concrete changes to improve our lives. Thinking about life with the end in mind is a powerful lens for reverse-engineering the decisions we make, so we will have fewer regrets when we look back.

The global trauma of the Covid-19 pandemic has done this at a societal level. People are asking foundational questions about how to make institutions like healthcare and education more effective, humane, and equitable. Even the number of hours the average person should work—and especially from where!—is being reevaluated. This broader reckoning with our lifestyles is one of the silver linings of this tragic, traumatic chapter in the world's history, because it provides us with the possibility of a paradigm shift for the better, a chance to hit the reset button.

Faced with so much suffering and death, ordinary people are taking stock of their lives and what is truly important to them. This is an opportunity for us to shift gears on both a personal and collective level and to become wiser decision-makers, as we are reminded that life can not only *end* at any moment, it can also radically *change* at any moment due to circumstances beyond our control.

IN MY WORK as an Emotional Health Counselor, we do an exercise that I call the value-time-spent chart. We write down our current values in one column and put the amount of time we spend on them in a second column. For example, one person I worked with wrote that "spending time with my family" was one of her values, but then wrote in the second column that she only spent 30 minutes over breakfast with them before rushing to her first Zoom meeting. This allowed her to see that the time she was spending wasn't in alignment with how much she valued her family. She could then think about how she might modify her schedule to make more time for them. This part of the process requires a great deal of honesty with oneself; she realized that she wasn't willing to give up her evening yoga class, because that brought great value to her life, too. She ended up deciding to look for a different job with more flexible hours so she could pick her children up from school and spend time with them several afternoons a week. In this way, she consciously and deliberately changed her life circumstances to align with her values.

Another way we can look at our values is to make the distinction between "have-to" values—things our parents or our culture have taught us we should value and spend our time on—and "want-to" values—things we have chosen on our own and not taken on from our parents or surroundings. It is surprising how many people have never thought about their own "want-to" values or even realized that there is a difference between what they want and what they have been told they want—and there usually is a difference.

One example of a "have-to" value that is rarely questioned is the value of having children. Many people are raised with the expectation from their parents and society as a whole that they will have children; often, having a family is presented as an inevitable, obvious stage of life. But when people accept having children as a default decision, they can end up being unhappy parents—possibly without even realizing why. After all, it is taboo to admit, even to yourself, that your life might be more fulfilled without children once you already have them. And when people end up as parents without asking themselves if it's truly what they want, they are not the only ones who suffer unhappiness: their children can end up feeling resented and unwanted.

It isn't easy to reject "have-to" values. Even when we are aware that they don't line up with our "want-to" values, we risk disappointing and alienating our parents or others in our lives who feel personally invested in our choices. Just think about how many couples end up having elaborate wedding receptions that they don't actually want, because their parents insist on it! However, it is well worth pushing past the fear of rejection or anger that comes with asserting our own "want-to" values. The more we cave in to "have-to" values, the less we are living our own truths. When we are honest about how we truly want to live, even when it leads to difficult conversations, we live joyfully and fulfilled. And, most importantly, with fewer regrets at the end. Whenever that is.

Since I began doing end-of-life care, I have learned to focus on what I value and devote my time and energy to those things.

REVIVING THE LOST ART OF GRIEVING

IT IS IMPOSSIBLE to talk about rethinking one's life and values without addressing the importance of grieving. In fact, grieving is the gateway to implementing the core of what the dying teach us: to live fully. It is a catalyst.

Loss in a Culture that Denies Grief

But why is it so difficult for us to grieve? To openly show this emotion that is an integral part of us, like all other emotions? Why have we lost the ways to express our sadness over the losses we experience — as we all experience loss, sooner or later, in one way or another?

In many ancient cultures, people used to grieve and mourn extensively, with all kinds of rituals and in community. However, this tradition has been sacrificed on the altar of our modern, technology-driven societies, where the future is being created through the lens of technology but not humanity. Death and the resulting sense of loss are the last remaining boundaries in an otherwise totally unbounded time.

Even though everyone grieves differently—and this emotion is felt at a different intensity for each person—like death itself, grief makes us uncomfortable. We don't want to be reminded that grief is an integral part of life, because with all our medical progress, we have ceased to accept death. And this is the reason why mourning a loss is viewed as something unpleasant, unwanted, and unnatural in modern society. Grief is covered in shame, considered a weakness and a failure. No wonder, since with grieving nothing is being produced. There is no measureable progress to be made. As the Chinese writer and doctor Christine Li wrote in the book *The Path of the Empress*, "mourning is the allowing—the very letting happen—of pain in the face of destruction and end. It is passive. It is the total surrender to nothingness." But in today's societies, we are expected to do the opposite: to restore our functionality and our productivity as quickly as possible. Hence, we are supposed to simply "overcome" the loss in private and "move on" as soon as we can.

DURING THE DECADE I have spent with the dying, I naturally have forged connections with their surviving dependents. Even though the "job" of a hospice worker is technically over after the funeral, it never has been for me. When it is your job at the deathbed to encourage a father to ask his son for forgiveness and say goodbye to him, or to encourage a daughter to put one last cigarette into her mother's mouth for her to savor, or to make it clear to someone who is in denial that they will never have the chance to hold their beloved partner's hand unless they do it now, you connect with them on the most existential, human level.

I found that, as I stayed in touch with these bereaved family members and friends, they were often left alone with no real space in which to grieve their loss. The loved ones I kept in touch with after their loss were emotionally constipated, unable to express the depth of their pain, and I wanted to be able to help them.

This inspired me to become an Emotional Health Counselor specializing in grief work. I took a training course, got certified as a professional coach by IPEC (the Institute for Professional Excellence in Coaching), and created my own grieving methodology.

My Epiphany: Grief is Gold

Not long after I started doing this work, I had an epiphany: Grieving is so much more than just releasing the emotion itself so we can regain the life energy we had before our loss. No, grieving is much more powerful. It holds the potential for great inner transformation. Done properly, it has a life-changing effect. We will not be the same as we were before.

When we give ourselves permission to grieve, we give ourselves permission to become comfortable with the vulnerable, wounded beings we all are inside. Yes, we *all* are! It's just that we cover it up with all sorts of different layers of artifice. As scary as grief work feels in the beginning, it is a truly healing experience and utterly rewarding. Believe me, I have done it.

First and foremost, having the courage to feel pain, to cry, to truly mourn what we have lost, is the number one doorway back to our truest selves—and as a consequence, to others. All of a sudden, we become able to connect with others around us on a more profound level than ever before and develop unprecedented closeness. Grief reunites us. It rebuilds communion and community. And isn't that what we need to do anyway?

Secondly, it has a powerful cleansing effect. Just as we cleanse our bodies from the outside, grieving cleanses our souls from the inside. It is an exhausting process, but as it progresses, it refills us with an indescribable energy of fullness, consciousness, and clarity. And it is in that transcendence when the new can arise, and we feel how we can create from a more powerful place than before.

Ultimately, when we stop sidestepping grief but choose to move through it, we allow ourselves to deepen and ripen. To see life through the lens of its essence. It is from that new inner place that we can then focus on redefining and realigning our values, diminishing our regrets, and living with a deepened sense of meaning.

Grief, this unwanted emotion, has the power to deeply transform us. It is gold.

Dare to Grieve — Now More Than Ever

In fact, there are many kinds of losses other than the death of a beloved person. There is also the loss of a relationship, the loss of a home or homeland, the loss of one's culture, the loss of our planet, the loss of a business, a pet, or even an object.

With my grieving methodology, I use grieving rituals (both indoors and in nature), value realignment exercises, and regret diminishing tools. It fills me with great joy and gratitude to see how, each time after going through an active grieving process, individuals and families indeed make wiser decisions and hence diminish their regrets.

A couple I worked with thought they wanted a divorce. However, when I asked them to write their obituaries as if they would die tomorrow, like I had done during my end-of-life caregiver training, they both realized that they would deeply regret it if they separated. They decided to stay together and help each other grow through the tough times they were facing and ended up happier and more deeply connected than they were before.

One successful entrepreneur I worked with wanted to create a legacy other than money. I asked him to imagine lying on his deathbed, and he realized that, at that point in his life, not a single family member or friend would come to his bedside, because he was not close with anyone. After that, he began a process to repair his relationships with his family by starting to talk to them again. They went to family therapy and rebuilt their connections based on honesty and compassion.

I believe that grieving is more important now than ever, because it is a gateway to creating a world in which we can be human again. And this is what the world badly needs right now. Western culture demands that we always show up positive, that we portray ourselves as constantly "making progress" towards more happiness, but we are doing this at the cost of storing our repressed emotions, such as sadness, fear, shame, and anger, even deeper within ourselves. When we deny these emotions, we deny half of what makes us human.

But when we dare to grieve, when we find the courage to befriend this dark emotion inside of us, we integrate all parts of ourselves. Let's revive the art of grieving and become whole. As a result, we make wiser decisions, one at a time, for ourselves and thus for others as well.

This is the very point of departure from which we can heal and begin restoring this wonderful world.

ACKNOWLEDGMENTS

First, I would like to honor the many people who confided to me, during personal conversations, how they viewed their lives in retrospect and how they wished to be remembered. It was a privilege to witness that and I am so appreciative of their trust in me.

I am extremely grateful to the nurses and doctors who made it possible for me to speak with people dying of Covid-19. For these patients, there was no time for hospice, and my heartfelt praise goes out to all those who cared for them in their final moments. These healthcare workers brought as much compassion and humanity as they could to their patients under the most inhumane circumstances.

I am greatly indebted to the many doctors, nurses, and staff members at hospices, nursing homes, and hospitals who made it possible to visit their patients as they neared the end of their lives. In the many facilities I visited, I encountered staff who were exceptionally friendly, patient, and empathetic, from the administrators to the cleaning staff. I have the highest regard for what they accomplish in our society every day.

Thanks also to everyone who helped me produce this book at light speed: Elisabeth Lauffer and Edna McCown for translating my writing from the original German, Susan Shankin for design and publication, Deborah Steinberg for developmental editing, and Julie Simpson for copyediting.

And I extend a special thank-you to Leslie Thurman, Director of Global Programming at the Milken Institute, for inviting me to speak at the Milken Institute's 24th annual Global Conference as part of the session "Healing the Trauma of Our Time: Permission to Grieve and Heal," and for creating this forum to acknowledge the importance of grief.

RECOMMENDED READING

Barnes, Julian. *Nothing to Be Frightened Of.* New York: Vintage, 2009.

Didion, Joan. *The Year of Magical Thinking.* New York: Vintage, 2007.

Halifax, Joan. *Being with Dying: Cultivating Compassion and Fearlessness in the Presence of Death.* Boulder: Shambhala Publications, 2009.

Kübler-Ross, Elisabeth. *Living with Death and Dying: How to Communicate with the Terminally Ill.* New York: Scribner, 1997.

Kübler-Ross, Elisabeth. *On Death and Dying: What the Dying Have to Teach Doctors, Nurses, Clergy & Their Own Families.* New York: Scribner, 2014.

Li, Christine and Ulja Krautwald. *The Path of the Empress: How to Free Your Feminine Power.* New South Wales: Rockpool Publishing, 2015.

Miller, BJ and Shoshana Berger. *A Beginner's Guide to the End. How to Live Life to the Full and Die a Good Death.* London: Quercus Books, 2019.

Rinpoche, Sogyal. *The Tibetan Book of Living and Dying.* San Francisco: Harper San Francisco, 2020.

Trunga, Chögyam and Francesca Fremantle. *The Tibetan Book of the Dead.* Boulder: Shambhala Publications, 2000.

Weller, Francis. *The Wild Edge of Sorrow: Rituals of Renewal and the Sacred Work of Grief.* Berkeley: North Atlantic Books, 2015.

ABOUT THE AUTHOR

CHRISTIANE ZU SALM is an Emotional Health Counselor, author, speaker, creator, and the host of the podcast *Before It's Too Late*. A former media executive for MTV Networks and IAC, she also served as a senior advisor to JP Morgan.

Christiane is a trained end-of-life caretaker and certified professional IPEC coach. After a decade of hospice work, she now specializes in grief counseling. In her virtual practice, she teaches accomplished entrepreneurs who feel stuck, burned out, or empty inside how to grieve losses of any kind so they can reconnect to themselves, diminish their regrets, and find sustained meaning in their lives.

She holds an MBA with distinction from Ludwig-Maximilians-Universität in Munich, Germany.

Website:	christianezusalm.com
LinkedIn:	linkedin.com/in/christianezusalm
Instagram:	#christianezusalm
Podcast:	*Before It's Too Late* on Apple Podcasts, Spotify, Google Podcasts
Email:	office@christianezusalm.com

Milton Keynes UK
Ingram Content Group UK Ltd.
UKHW050026280324
440135UK00005B/14/J